Original title:
Frostbite Fiasco

Author: Zachary Prescott
ISBN HARDBACK: 978-9916-94-322-9
ISBN PAPERBACK: 978-9916-94-323-6

Veil of Crystal Frost

In a winter wonderland with icy glee,
Snowflakes tumble like they’re on spree.
Penguins skate in their oversized hats,
Slipping and sliding like playful acrobats.

A snowman grins with a carrot nose,
But his twig arms wave as a chill blows.
He falls apart with a frosty sigh,
As kids giggle, oh my, oh my!

Icicles hang like a glistening crown,
While dogs chase flakes and tumble down.
They spin in circles, licking the air,
As snowballs fly without a care.

Winter’s a riot with laughter galore,
Hot cocoa spills as we slip on the floor.
With frostbitten toes and noses too red,
We can't stop laughing until we're in bed.

Chill in the Air

Penguins dance as they slip and slide,
Snowflakes tumble, nowhere to hide.
Hot cocoa spills on the frosty ground,
Laughter echoes, a merry sound.

Scarves unravel, hats fly away,
Snowball battles brighten the day.
Mittens clashing, colors absurd,
In the winter fun, we all feel stirred.

Whispering Ice Trails

Sleds go zooming, a chaotic race,
Wipeouts happen—it's all part of grace.
Ice skates wobble on the glistening lake,
Each graceful fall is a giggly mistake.

Snowmen topple with a gentle thud,
Top hats lost in a snowy flood.
Chilly breezes bring giggles and cheer,
Creating stories we hold so dear.

Shivers of the Heart

A chill runs down as I step outside,
In puffy jackets, we all try to hide.
With noses red and cheeks aglow,
We freeze together in this frosty show.

A snowball flies, it lands on a friend,
The laughter erupts, it won't ever end.
In this icy kingdom, we thrive with glee,
In every stumble, pure joy we see.

The Frozen Misstep

On the icy sidewalk, I take a chance,
One little slip and I'm in a dance!
With arms flailing wildly, I make a scene,
Winter's ballet, oh, it's quite the fiend!

Fallen mittens, a picture so bright,
Giggling friends turn my fumble to flight.
In chilly chaos, we find our way,
As laughter and snowflakes brighten the day.

Whispers of the Frozen Wind

A snowman lost his nose today,
He says he’ll look for it on delay.
With carrot dreams and frosty breath,
He shuffles on, defying death.

Behind the trees, the owls all hoot,
While squirrels wear their fluffy suit.
They scatter nuts with chilly glee,
And giggle at the frosty spree.

In the Hour of Ice

Icicles hang like teeth from a smile,
Yet slips and falls are all the style.
With each step, a ballet of grace,
We wobble and tumble, a slippery race.

Hot cocoa spills, it's quite a shame,
As mugs of joy become a game.
Marshmallows float like frozen ships,
Sail on the froth of our frozen trips.

Riddles of the Winter Storm

A penguin in a misplaced hat,
Dances with a kangaroo—imagine that!
Snowflakes giggle at the sight,
While the sun peeks out, oh what a fright!

Jack Frost plays tricks, oh he is sly,
As icicles twinkle like stars in the sky.
We sing and freeze, a merry band,
In this wild, wintry wonderland.

The Frozen Frontier

Snowball fights like battles bold,
Covered in layers, we shiver and scold.
But laughter rings loud in the cold air,
As we share our warmth, show we care.

A harmony of laughter, crisp and bright,
While snowflakes swirl in a playful flight.
The frozen ground is our silly stage,
As winter writes its comical page.

The Chill's Awakening

The winter winds began to howl,
Snowflakes danced with a cheeky scowl.
My nose turned red, my toes went numb,
Oh, what fun in icy blunder!

A penguin slid right past my face,
In snowball fights, we lost all grace.
Slipping here and tumbling there,
Laughter echoes in the frigid air!

Heart of the Frozen Abyss

In the depths of winter's reach,
Hilarity became my frosty speech.
My hot cocoa promptly froze,
Who knew it could be so comatose?

A snowman grinned with carrot nose,
But stumbled when the evening froze.
He toppled down with a hearty crash,
And all around, we giggled in a flash!

Tales from the Icy Edge

In frozen realms where laughter sings,
I danced with joy on frosted wings.
But alas, my boots went slip and slide,
And down I went with arms flung wide!

Snowdrifts covered my gleeful face,
As I discovered winter's embrace.
With each attempt to stand up tall,
I laughed out loud and took a fall!

Frosted Memories

With mittens lost and scarves in knots,
We built a fort with all our thoughts.
Snowballs flying, friends galore,
It’s a winter's joke we can't ignore!

Chilly cheeks and giggles bright,
As snowflakes twirled in frosty light.
The cold may nip, but hearts stay warm,
In every freeze, we find our charm!

Heartbreak in the Cold

I slipped on ice, oh what a sight,
My heart skidded into the night.
Love's warmth vanished in the frost,
Now I'm stuck, what a cost!

Chipper squirrels mock my plight,
While I flail in pure delight.
My date abandoned, laughed and rolled,
Now I'm freezing, feeling old.

With snowflakes falling, fresh and bright,
I ponder love that's out of sight.
Laughter echoes, a winter's tease,
Next time I'll wear shoes with ease.

Frosted Dreams

In winter’s grip, I dream aloud,
Of toasty nights and blankets proud.
Instead, I nipped by icy cheer,
A polar bear just sneered, oh dear!

My cocoa's cold, it lost its heat,
Like my ambition, beat by sleet.
I wrap my scarf and hum a tune,
While penguins plot the next monsoon.

The snowman winks, it clears his throat,
Says winter's charm ain’t worth a vote.
I fall down laughing in this mess,
Next time I’ll bring my thermal dress.

The Perilous Snowfall

As flakes arrive like little spies,
I walk the street with frosty sighs.
A slip, a tumble, oh what grace,
I challenge igloos to a race!

The snowball fights erupt in glee,
While mittens stick to my right knee.
If life’s a dance, I missed the beat,
Just call me ‘Mr. Slippery Feet’!

Then here comes a snowplow, loud and proud,
With a honk that draws a laughing crowd.
I bow to the avalanche ahead,
Guess making friends while stooped is red.

Chilling Encounters

Met a snowman with a crooked hat,
He claimed he’s cooler than a cat.
We chatted ‘til the sun peeked through,
Now he’s a puddle, poor dear too.

Frosty winds play a chilly game,
While penguins waltz, I feel the shame.
With every gust, my hair’s a fright,
Fashion’s fun when it’s frozen tight!

Yet laughter lingers in the air,
Moments shared, without a care.
I’ll cherish each frosty silly fling,
In winter heart, I’ll make ’em sing.

Frozen Fractures

In the land of ice and snow,
Jokes slip and slide, oh no!
With frozen toes, we dance and play,
Laughter echoes, come what may.

Snowmen wobble, hats askew,
A carrot nose that's slightly askew.
The sun peeks out, a cheeky grin,
We cheer and shout, let the fun begin!

Slipping, sliding, down we go,
On icy paths, it's quite the show!
With every tumble, giggles grow,
Mirth and madness, a winter glow.

Heartbeats in Winter

Winter's chill makes hearts race fast,
With every snowball fight, we laugh.
Jumping high, we seek the skies,
In puffy jackets, silly, we rise.

Footprints stampede on icy ground,
Each step a crunching, joyful sound.
With frosty breath, we share a cheer,
Winter's quirks bring folks near.

Giggles flow as snowflakes fall,
A dance party at the mall!
Hot cocoa spills, marshmallows fly,
In winter's grip, we reach for the sky.

Dance of the Shivering Shadows

Shadows dance in the pale moonlight,
Wobbling shapes that give a fright.
Grab your mittens, it's time to sway,
To the silly tunes of a frosty play.

With gloved hands, we twist and twirl,
A chilly dance that makes us whirl.
Each step a slide, whoops, there we go,
Laughter ringing through the snow!

The moon winks down, a frosty cheer,
Our twitching toes can't feel the fear.
We slide and spin, with cheerful shouts,
In the snowy night, joy sprouts.

Beneath the Crystalline Veil

Under a blanket, soft and white,
Noses red, a funny sight.
Snowflakes tickle, a gentle tease,
Tickling laughter on winter's breeze.

Icicles dangle like frozen swords,
Defending forts with friendly hoards.
With snowballs flying, we create a mess,
Each playful hit, a jovial jest.

Hot soup awaits, a cozy treat,
Warming up our frosty feet.
Beneath the frost, laughter swells,
In this season, all is well!

Beneath the Chill’s Embrace

A penguin slipped on icy ground,
With flippers flailing all around.
He landed hard, his face in snow,
And laughed aloud, ‘Oh, what a show!’

A snowman grinned with carrot stout,
Its arms were branches, there's no doubt.
But when the wind gave him a spin,
He lost his hat and shouted, ‘Win!’

Children bundled for a play,
Tumbling down, they find their way.
But mittens lost, and socks unfound,
Joke about the frosty ground!

The hot cocoa’s gone quite cold,
Yet stories of adventure told.
As snowflakes dance, all in a whirl,
Life’s icy moments make us twirl.

When Silence Freezes

The garden statue goes for walks,
In winter's grip, he never talks.
But one brave squirrel took a leap,
Challenged the chill, and made us weep.

A quiet crunch beneath our feet,
The sound of ice, a funny beat.
We tried to skate, but oh, the fail,
Slipped into snow like fish on scale.

Laughter echoed in the freeze,
As jackets flapped in the brisk breeze.
We built a fort, but lost the fight,
When kids attacked with snowballs bright.

Even the ice could not contain,
The silly antics driven insane.
Through frozen days, we'll keep on jest,
In shivers, we find our very best.

The Iceness Within

A cat once thought it could not fall,
On icy paths, it spied a ball.
With one swift paw, it made its claim,
But soon found out, it played a game.

Hot chocolate sipping by the fire,
While snowflakes dance with pure desire.
Then cheery tales of winter woes,
Flood in our hearts as laughter flows.

A pair of gloves now lost to time,
A story told, it feels like rhyme.
Oh, how the frost can play a part,
In warming up a cold, cold heart!

The chilly air brings tales to tell,
Of snowmen plots, they know so well.
Through every slip and stumble made,
We find the fun that never fades.

Screams Beneath the Snow

A child took off down the hill,
He soared—and landed with a thrill.
But oh, the snow, it pulled him down,
And left him flailing without a frown.

A winter's tale of sledding dreams,
As laughter bounces, or so it seems.
The necktie twirled around like twine,
With voices echoing in their rhyme.

Snowballs launched like little bombs,
Our giggles mixed with winter's psalms.
Grown-ups throw and duck and dive,
In this frosty fray, we feel alive!

But as the day begins to fade,
And all our shenanigans displayed,
We bundle up, with cheeks aglow,
Warmed by the fun beneath the snow.

The Bitter Side of Winter

Snowflakes swirl with swirling glee,
The ground is slick, oh not for me.
A slip, a slide, a comical fall,
Winter's here, but it’s a ball!

Hats on heads like puffy balloons,
Warmth escapes like playful tunes.
Laughter echoes in the cold,
As hot chocolate stories unfold.

Shivers dance, my nose turns red,
Ice on sidewalks, my shoes I dread.
But with a laugh and bright warm smiles,
We'll conquer winter’s silly trials.

So let it snow, let the winds blow,
With mittens on, we’ll dance, you know.
For every chill that bites our skin,
A giggle bridges where warmth begins.

Frosted Footprints

Footprints dotted on the white,
Like a clown’s shoes in morning light.
Slipping here and slipping there,
Winter's prank, but I don’t care!

Eager to build a snowman tall,
With a crooked grin, and a floppy shawl.
His carrot nose took a dive, oh dear,
He’s wobbly, but brings us cheer!

Snowball fights, oh what a thrill,
Until someone takes a spill!
Rolling in the snow so bright,
Winter fun brings such delight.

As chilly winds begin to bite,
We warm our hearts with pure delight.
In frosty footprints, laughter lingers,
Winter holds us with snowy fingers.

A Perilous Chill

Outdoors I venture, oh what a scene,
Can’t feel my toes, but my smile is keen.
A shiver sends a jolt up my spine,
Yet a hearty laugh is simply divine!

My scarf's a flag in a frosty war,
Hilarious happens, who could ask for more?
A neighbor’s snowman leans to one side,
As the snowflakes gather for a ride.

Sipping soup like it’s molten gold,
The spicy warmth breaks winter’s cold.
But oops! I dropped it - oh what a sight,
A splash of broth, oh what a fright!

Snow vests look silly with too much fluff,
Dressed like marshmallows, that’s just enough.
With chilly smiles and breath in steam,
We laugh at the icy winter's dream.

Bound by Ice

Trapped in layers, I shuffle so slow,
Icicles dangle, putting on a show.
Each step I take sounds like a crack,
Watch me waddle, there’s no turning back!

Around the corner, the snowmen stand,
With crooked top hats, they’re looking grand.
But oh! My hat flies off in the wind,
As laughter erupts, winter’s best friend.

A frozen lake, a daredevil glide,
But oh dear me, I just can’t abide!
Down I go with a squishy thump,
Where did my balance go? Oh what a lump!

So here we are, cuddled so tight,
Fixing funny glows in the night.
Winter wraps us, a frosty embrace,
With laughs and fun in this chilly place.

Icicle Serenade

Beneath the eaves, they dangle long,
Shimmering notes to winter's song.
A slippery slip, a jolly fall,
Who knew ice could sing at all?

Chasing secrets, with laughter loud,
A snowball fight, in the middle of a crowd.
But with one wrong step, the giggles stop,
As icicles perform a comical flop!

The dog dances, with paws akimbo,
While grandma twirls, in her fur-lined limbo.
Each frozen shard, a tiny spear,
Yet we can't help but cheer and cheer!

So raise a cup of hot cocoa cheer,
For frosty mischief draws us near.
In a winter wonderland, wild and bright,
Even the cold can’t freeze our light.

Frozen Footprints

In the snow, prints weave and dart,
Each one a tale, a snowy art.
Who stepped where? A mystery game,
Let’s trace them back—who’s to blame?

A bunny hops, with a wiggly nose,
While the neighbor's cat strikes a pose.
But wait! What's that? A slip and slide,
A comical crash—oh, how we cried!

The path is a comedic ballet,
With flailing arms, we sway and sway.
One step forward, two steps back,
As we navigate this frosty track.

Laughter erupts, as snowflakes twirl,
Each stumble turns into a whirl.
In this frozen dance, we'll find delight,
Our footprints telling stories, oh so bright!

Winter’s Wager

A bet was placed on who’d get cold,
With winter's chill, it quickly rolled.
A scarf too short, a hat too tight,
Fashion disaster, what a sight!

The neighbor's dog, a furry clown,
Bounding through drifts, tumbling down.
With every trip, a yappy cheer,
He’s the champion of winter's sphere!

Hot chocolate wagers warming hands,
While mittens melt into snowy lands.
We shake on it, as flurries dance,
Who’d thought we’d end in a snowball prance!

And as we tally losses gained,
With every giggle, joy remained.
So here’s to bets in icy air,
Where laughter’s warmth is everywhere!

The Edge of Cold Reality

Winter whispers secrets cold,
Promises wrapped in layers bold.
But one misstep, and lo and behold,
Reality’s edge is a slippery fold!

A charming snowman stands so proud,
Until a warm breeze pokes through the crowd.
His carrot nose begins to droop,
As giggles explode in a frosty group!

A sledge ride ends with a splash,
In a puddle, a glorious crash.
With snowflakes flying, we shout and grin,
Winter's fun is where we begin!

So embrace the cold, let laughter be,
For humor blooms in the frost we see.
To dance on ice, and tumble around,
In this wacky winter, joy abounds!

Bewitched by the Cold

I stepped outside with glee and cheer,
But my nose turned red, oh dear, oh dear!
The snowflakes danced, they caught my hat,
I spun around, then slipped like a cat.

My boots were laced with icy dread,
I thought I'd glide, but I instead
Landed flat with a comic thud,
While snowmen laughed and waved, oh crud!

With mittens thick and scarf so wide,
I waddled like a penguin, full of pride.
The chili in my cup was good and hot,
But spilled it all—oh, what a lot!

Now every time it starts to freeze,
I wear my gear like a fashion tease.
I'll dance with frost, I won't be shy,
Just as long as I don’t fly!

The Winter's Bane

The snow fell thick, my cheeks were bright,
I tried to make a snowman right.
But as I packed the icy flake,
It collapsed—oh, what a mistake!

I tossed some snow to start a ball,
But it rolled away, I watched it fall.
Down the hill, it gathered speed,
It knocked me over—it was a deed!

With every step, a crunch and slip,
I looked like I was on a trip.
My friends all cheered, "You're a pro!"
But I was buried, beneath the snow!

Then came the wind, it howled and blew,
My hat flew off, oh what to do?
Chasing it madly, I was a sight,
Defeated by winter—or was it fright?

Interlude in the Ice

The pond was frozen, a lovely sight,
I laced my skates, it felt just right.
But one small slip and whoosh! I'm down,
I flailed my arms like a flopping clown.

My friends all giggled, pointing, too,
As I attempted a fancy move, woohoo!
With every spin, I found my fate,
My graceful glide turned into a crate.

A wind gust blew, my scarf took flight,
It danced and twirled, a comical sight.
I chased it, ran, what a big faux pas,
I slipped and landed—au revoir, ta-ta!

Now every time I lace up tight,
I think of that day and laugh with delight.
Embracing the ice, I take a bow,
At least I tried, I'll figure it out somehow!

Shadows of a Winter Tale

The shadows grew as daylight fled,
I clutched my cocoa, felt quite fed.
My blanket wrapped, I touched my nose,
Outside the chilly winter blows!

A snowball fight erupted fast,
I dodged and ducked, but alas, alas!
A flying snowball hit my face,
I fell backwards—what a disgrace!

With laughter ringing in the air,
I pranced like I didn't care.
But every snowdrift called my name,
As I slipped again—what a game!

So here's to winter, laughter and cheer,
May our frozen adventures be held dear.
With each frosty jest and playful fall,
We'll brave the cold, winter's enthrall!

Challenges in the Snow

A snowman wearing my old hat,
He teeters and wobbles, oh, imagine that!
I slipped on ice, my legs took flight,
Landed in a snowdrift, what a funny sight!

The sled dog team is on a stroll,
But they chase my scarf, out of control!
Snowflakes tickle my nose and then,
I sneeze so loud, I scare the hen!

Chasing my gloves, they dance so free,
Like little furballs, can’t catch them, whee!
With every step, I’m a comedy show,
Sliding down the hill, how fast can I go?

Winter’s charm is a slapstick play,
Where we laugh and fumble all the way.
Snowmen giggle as we tumble too,
Oh, the joys of slipping with my crew!

The Iced Chronicle

Once upon a time, the ice was sly,
It took my balance — oh, oh my!
With every crack, my heart would beat,
On a frozen pond, I danced on my feet!

My cup of cocoa slipped from hand,
Splashing a snowman, wasn't that grand?
He blinked and melted, what a drama,
I ran away, calling it bad karma!

Around the corner, a snowball fight,
My aim was off, hit a tree, how bright!
Down it tumbled, branches creaked,
I guess that branch was just too weak!

Ice skates squeaking with every glide,
I look like a duck on a joyride!
Fall on my tail, it's quite a scene,
Winter's tales in a comical sheen!

Beneath the Arctic Sun

Beneath the glow of a wintry sun,
We laugh and frolic, winter fun begun!
A penguin slips, I swear I saw,
As he fell backward, in awe I guffaw!

With marshmallow hats, we strut around,
Making big footprints, all over town.
A hot chocolate avalanche spoils my smile,
Sprayed on my buddy, oh, what a style!

Snowball missiles ready to soar,
But I threw mine and hit a door!
The folks inside burst out in glee,
Winter's a party, can't disagree!

At twilight, laughter rings through the air,
While penguins parade without any care.
Under the icy glow, we beam with pride,
In a world of wonder, let's take a slide!

Shadows of the Winter Sky

In shadows cast by the winter trees,
I pranced around, slipped with ease.
A snowflake waltzed down my nose,
I shook my head, it bid me close!

With every step, I sway and twirl,
But like a top, I start to swirl!
Down the slope, without a plan,
I bump a snowman, oh man, oh man!

Icicles dance like little pranks,
When one drops down, I give my thanks!
For laughter shared all on this land,
In winter's grasp, we take our stand!

As shadows grow long and the sun sets low,
The giggles and slips put on quite a show.
We cheer the moon, with snowflakes around,
In this winter tale, joy does abound!

Glacial Melodies

The snowman danced with winter's glee,
His carrot nose a sight to see.
With frigid tunes, he took a spin,
While snowflakes laughed, a waltz to win.

His buddy slipped upon the ice,
A pratfall, oh! It’s not that nice.
But giggles rang through the chilly air,
As frosty friends forgot their care.

A penguin skated, arms held wide,
Across the rink, he took a ride.
Yet tripped on snowball, made a mess,
Landing right in winter's dress!

But laughter echoed through the trees,
As snowballs flew like buzzing bees.
In this cold world where chaos reigns,
The joy of winter humor gains.

Thorns of the Winter's Rage

There once was a cactus clad in frost,
Who bitterly mourned what he had lost.
His prickly friends could barely stand,
As icicles dripped from every brand.

A blizzard blew with a sneezy sound,
While lumps of snow sat all around.
The struggles of those icy thorns,
Made them lament, those winter scorns.

But laughter sparked in frozen lands,
As penguins plotted their funny plans.
They piled up snow in a silly fight,
While thorns just chuckled at the sight.

So let the wind whip wild and fierce,
We'll make snow angels, our hearts it pierce.
In thorns of winter, joy will flow,
For in the cold, our spirits glow.

Echoes of a Frigid Heart

A snowflake whispered to a star,
'Why do we twinkle from afar?'
The star just chuckled, 'Some lose their way,
In winter’s grip, we dance and sway.'

A penguin moaned at the frozen sea,
'Oh, where’s the warmth? Let me be free!'
His buddy laughed, 'Just keep your cool,
In dreams of summer, you’ll rule the pool!'

The frost grew bold, with a sassy cheer,
For it knew that laughter was always near.
In icy realms where hearts are bright,
Echoes of joy twinkle in the night.

So if one stumbles on snow's embrace,
Let giggles ring out, no time to race.
For even in cold, love still imparts,
Warmth like sunshine in frigid hearts.

Shard of the Bitter Night

In midnight's grasp, the chill did bite,
A snowman sighed, 'What a plight!'
His hat askew, he frowned and thought,
'Is this the warmth that I had sought?'

While icicles hung like jaded teeth,
A squirrel zipped by, full of mischief beneath.
He squeaked with glee at a frosty prank,
While snowflakes danced, as if in a bank.

The night was filled with giggles and gaffes,
As winter's troupe rehearsed their laughs.
One slip, one slide, oh what a scene,
Frosty capers like a slapstick dream!

Yet when dawn broke with a timid grin,
The laughter echoed from within.
For in this cold, we found our light,
Shard of joy on a bitter night.

Deputy of the Winter’s Chill

In a coat so thick it grew quite stout,
The deputy waddled, without a doubt.
Snowflakes danced upon his head,
He sneezed so loud, the snowflakes fled!

With icicles hanging off his chin,
He tried to twirl but took a spin.
Seeking warmth in hot cocoa's embrace,
He spilled it all; what a frosty disgrace!

The town folks laughed at his silly plight,
As he slipped and slid into the bright.
Each step a shuffle, each breath a puff,
His frosty antics were quite enough!

But in the end, with a warm cup in hand,
He grinned and said, “Winter's just grand!”
Waddle we must, through winter so bright,
The deputy chuckles deep in the night!

Journey Through the Frosted Veil

A path of ice that crackled sweet,
Two friends set off, their shoes on fleet.
With every step a tiny crunch,
They laughed aloud, their warmth a punch!

But then a slip, and oh, what fun!
One tumbled down, the other spun.
Rolling like snowballs, giggles loud,
They made a frost-capped, giggling crowd!

Through trees so white, they danced with glee,
A waltz on ice, so carefree.
But watch your step, or you might fall,
And slide away, much to the thrall!

With hats of snow and gloves of frost,
They found it fun, never lost.
A journey shared, with laughter bright,
Through frosted veils, pure delight!

The Silent Frost

Whispers of snowfall, a blanket white,
The silent frost creeps in at night.
It giggles softly as branches sway,
Turning all to a winter ballet.

But when you step on the crunchy ground,
The frost can't hide, it laughs profound.
With squeaks and squeals beneath your feet,
It turns the chill into a warm treat!

A frost-kissed branch, so sly and bold,
Cracks a joke too, when stories are told.
It tickles the nose, and soon you sneeze,
As the frost dances in the frosty breeze!

In the morn, it giggles at each flake,
Reminding us of the fun we make.
So don your coat, take a frosty stand,
With laughter echoing through wintery land!

Cracks in the Ice

A lake so shiny, a winter's glass,
We slid around, like geese in class.
But watch your step, for it may crack,
And send us tumbling, what a whack!

Each jump a giggle, each slip a show,
We spun and twirled, our cheeks aglow.
Then whoops, a leap, then down we go,
Splashing ice water, what a show!

As frosted friends, we gather round,
In the snowy laughs, we're tightly bound.
Cracks in the ice, no cause for fret,
Just make a snowman, it’s a safe bet!

With carrots and smiles, we build our cheer,
Winter's fun brings us ever near.
So dance on ice, let worries flee,
In this winter world, just be carefree!

Slumbering in the Cold

A snowman dreams of sunny days,
With visions of summer's golden rays.
His carrot nose takes on a pout,
As winter winds start to shout.

A squirrel shivers in a fur coat tight,
Plotting schemes to steal a bite.
The frozen pond is quite the mess,
When ducks try skating in their dress.

Yet laughter echoes through the trees,
As frosty winds begin to tease.
A snowball flies, it strikes with cheer,
Transforms our sighs to fits of fear.

So gather round, don't take a chance,
With chilly winds, let’s start a dance.
We’ll waddle home through snowflakes bright,
And warm our hearts with silly plight.

Winter's Silent War

The icicles dangle, a pointy brigade,
They threaten an intruder, with icy trade.
Snowflakes whirl like a fluffy brigade,
In a battle of cold, let’s hope we’re not played!

The snow plow rumbles, a grumpy old man,
With dreams of a tropical sunbathing plan.
While kids with shovels wage war with glee,
And wish for a snowman that dances with me.

The frost bites noses, with a mischievous grin,
As dogs strengthen their bravery to challenge the din.
They frolic and tumble, while humans slip,
In this frosty tango, we all lose our grip.

Yet laughter erupts like bright shooting stars,
As mittens go flying; we dodge icy jars.
With every cold snap, the fun takes a lift,
In winter's wild war, we find our own gift.

The Enigma of the Frozen Ground

Beneath the surface, strange things lie,
A lost sock, a twig, and a rubber pie.
The ground sings secrets of chilly charm,
As we trudge over, hoping for warmth.

Snowdrifts hide treasures, or so I am told,
Like ancient tales of brave knights bold.
But all I find is a frozen shoe,
And a snowball aimed at my winter view.

The ground is a puzzle, a playful trap,
With footprints tracking, a slippery map.
Each step a riddle, each slip a laugh,
In this frozen game, we share a warm half.

So dance with the drifts, embrace the cold,
Join in the fun; let the story unfold.
With jests in the fray, let's wade and roam,
For in frozen antics, we find a home.

Wounds Beneath the Ice

Beneath the icy surface, a tale is spun,
Of penguins slipping, in a race for fun.
With every waddle, a giggle pops,
As flippers flail, and frostbit toes drop.

The pond is a stage for ballet gone wrong,
With chilly performers, we could write a song.
As they pirouette, and tumble down flat,
The ice gives a chuckle; 'Oh, fancy that!'

Laughter ensues as we gather around,
To witness the chaos that winter has found.
In jackets so puffy, we stumble and sway,
Yet find a new rhythm, as we laugh away.

So raise a warm mitt to the wintering scene,
For every slip echoes a joy unforeseen.
With wounds wrapped in laughter, and smiles that ignite,
We celebrate winter's paradoxical bite.

Crystals and Catastrophe

In winter's grip, I lost my shoe,
My toes are cold, what should I do?
With frozen feet, I dance in place,
A wobbly step, a silly face.

My friend slipped by, a sight to behold,
Down he went, it never gets old.
His flailing arms like a bird in flight,
A snowman chuckled at our plight.

Attempting to sled, we gave a cheer,
But crashed head-first, the end was near.
The snowbanks laughed as we tumbled down,
Two crazy kids in a silly town.

With frosty hair and frozen noses,
We braved the chill through frosty poses.
The laughter echoed through the night,
In icy madness, we found delight.

Glimmers in the Gloom

The shadows creep, the lights are dim,
But there’s a glow, a chance to skim.
I trip on ice, what a sight to see,
Like a slapstick film, all eyes on me.

A snowball fight erupts with glee,
I aim for you, but hit a tree.
The branches shake, a flurry of snow,
A blizzard of giggles begins to flow.

We twirl and spin, like whirling dervishes,
But land on our backs, it’s pure pernicious.
With laughter echoing beneath the stars,
We make frosty wishes on our chocolate bars.

The moonlight dances on the frozen ground,
While our silly antics and joy abound.
In winter's gloom, we find our way,
With every slip, we laugh and play.

Shadows of the Arctic Dance

In the chill of night, we bundle tight,
With hats askew, a comical sight.
We sway and shake, our boots too big,
A dance of shadows, all laughs and jig!

A rogue snowman winks from afar,
As we waddle past, our cheeks ajar.
A tumble here, a slip right there,
We pirouette in frosty air.

With icicles hanging like crooked teeth,
We laugh so hard, we can’t find breath.
Each spin and twirl, a partner in crime,
Oh, the joy of winter, it feels like prime time!

Yet as we bow, we hit the ground,
With snowflakes swirling all around.
In shadows thick, our giggles swell,
In this frigid chaos, all is well.

The Icebound Saga

Once upon a time in a frosty land,
I took a step, and things got out of hand.
I slipped and slid, like a penguin on ice,
My friends just laughed, oh isn't this nice?

A grand adventure in the frozen glade,
With frosty mustaches, we wielded our blades.
We built a fort made of snow and dreams,
To defend against marshmallows, or so it seems.

A snowball hit with a splat and a laugh,
Our witty banter, a cheeky gaffe.
The frozen air filled with joyous shouts,
In our winter world, we twirled about.

So here's to the chaos, to friendships anew,
In an icebound tale that's silly and true.
With every frosty giggle and cheer,
This saga of laughter will last all year.

A Rhapsody in White.

In winter's grip, a dance begins,
With snowflakes swirling, laughter spins.
A snowman wobbles, with a carrot hat,
His eyes all crooked, oh how he sat!

A penguin slips on ice, what a sight,
Flapping wings, oh what a fright!
This frosty romp, a joyous spree,
With friends all laughing, wild and free.

Snowballs flying, a winter's fling,
Watch out for that sneaky fling!
A tumble here, a giggle there,
Who knew cold could spark such flare?

When winter calls, we heed the sound,
In icy bliss, our joy is found.
With hot cocoa and hugs so tight,
We revel in this frosty night.

Chill of the Unseen

The air's so cold, it steals your breath,
Your nose turns red, could it be death?
Yet giggles burst like snowflakes fall,
In this frozen world, we'll have a ball!

A squirrel scurries, its tail a plume,
In snow-covered hills, there's laughter's room.
With cheeks aglow and spirits high,
Who knew cold could make us fly?

A slip on ice, a flailing flop,
But then a giggle, and we can't stop!
Belly laughs echo through the trees,
In this hidden world, we find our ease.

So let it snow, let it freeze,
We'll dance and prance with graceful ease.
For in the chill, we find our cheer,
In every frosty, funny sphere.

Whispers in the Snow

Soft whispers echo through the night,
As snowflakes tumble, pure delight.
A snowball rocks a quiet muse,
In this white wonderland, we cannot lose.

A dog jumps high, a frosty sprint,
Catching snowflakes, as they glint.
With each paw print, a story told,
Of chilly antics, bright and bold.

The icicles hang like frozen tears,
We laugh and tease, forget our fears.
With scarves and mittens, we shiver, sway,
In this comic ballet, hip-hip-hooray!

So gather round, our frosty crew,
In snowy realms, the laughter grew.
For every slip, a tale is spun,
A magical winter, for everyone!

The Icy Grip

The icy grip of winter's hug,
Makes us snuggle, gives a tug.
With mittens lost and noses red,
We tumble down, a snowy spread!

Snowflakes tickle, dancing around,
In this chilly chaos, we are bound.
A snow fort built, like castles grand,
Watch out! Here comes a flying hand!

Our breath fogs up, like dragon's fire,
While we build snowmen higher and higher.
Chasing laughter, we slip and glide,
In this frosty fun, we take great pride.

So let the winter do its worst,
We’ll face the chill, together burst.
In frozen moments, joy ignites,
With frosty fun, we share delights.

Snowbound Misadventure

In winter's grasp, we lost our way,
Our sledding dreams turned to dismay.
With frozen toes and cheeks aglow,
We giggled loud, as on we go.

The snowman waved with a nose of coal,
While icicles threatened our poor patrol.
A strawberry hat upon his head,
We found our madness, laughter spread.

The snow drifted like a fluffy sea,
Our lost mittens? Where could they be?
Jumping around like a leaf on fire,
In this crazy chill, we never tire.

But oh, dear friend, who tossed the snack?
It skidded away; we can't go back!
With shivers and giggles, we chase it down,
In this snowy mess, we wear our crown.

The Grasp of the Glacier

Alas, the glacier held us tight,
With icy fingers, a cheeky fright.
We tried to dance, but slipped and fell,
Laughter echoed; it rang like a bell.

A prankster seal swam near our feet,
Challenging us in this frosty feat.
We tossed him snacks; he rolled around,
Our frozen play turned to silly sound.

While snowflakes twirled in a swirling race,
We chased after dreams, in a merry place.
A snowball battle suddenly stalled,
With snowy laughter, we all recalled.

But watch out now; don't let it slide!
A hidden hill is where we tried.
We climbed back up with a loony cheer,
Only to tumble, so much to fear!

Misfortune Beneath the Snow

Beneath the snow, our boots did squish,
An unexpected, frosty mish.
With each step taken, we'd laugh and fall,
The icy pranksters snapped at all.

Crafting snow forts like pros in play,
Until an avalanche joined the fray.
While dodging drifts of white and fluff,
We found our laughter was quite enough.

The snowflakes whispered, 'Come join the fun,'
Yet every toss turned into a run.
Our gear was soaked, our spirits high,
The frosty winds made us cry.

We formed a line for a snowy slide,
One by one, what a bumpy ride!
From laughter loud to squeals of fright,
In this winter chaos, we took flight.

Cold Hands, Warm Desires

With cold hands busy, we built our dream,
A snow castle bright, or so it would seem.
But snowballs flew with a frosty grin,
Our ambitions fell, like ice wearing thin.

We wrapped our scarves, but still turned blue,
Each time we fell, we'd shout 'Who knew?'
The snow gave way, our hopes in despair,
We laughed and rolled without a care.

A snow queen waved with a frosty smile,
While we lost our balance in style.
Her laughter chimed, our hearts raced so,
We plotted revenge on the snowman below.

So here’s to winter, with all its chills,
We’ll take the frosts and snowy spills.
With winters brief and memories grand,
I’d trade it all for one warm hand.

Lament of the Winter Breeze

Oh, the chill that sneaks 'round the block,
With December's chill, I stand in shock.
My nose is pink, my fingers numb,
I jump and dance, oh what a fun crumb!

Neighbors cringe as I give a shout,
"Bundle up, before you head out!"
But still we laugh, as we slip and slide,
On icebergs in parks, we take pride.

The snowflakes twirl, oh what a sight,
But one caught my hat, a merry fright!
I chase it down, oh look at me,
A grown-up fool, on a snowy spree!

So here's to the frost, my frosty friend,
Causing shivers that never quite end.
We'll gather 'round, with cocoa so sweet,
And giggle at how we can't feel our feet.

Shivers of the Northern Wind

In the land where the snowflakes roam,
I lost my scarf, it feels like home!
The wind it howls, oh what a treat,
Whipping around my frozen feet.

In mittens too thick, I try to wave,
But my fingers are trapped, I can’t be brave!
I trip on snowbanks, a slip, a slide,
Laughter erupts, from the frozen tide.

Icicles hang like daggers in fright,
I shiver and giggle, it’s quite the sight.
I try to look tough, but look like a clown,
In layers of fluff, like a puff pastry gown!

So next time you freeze, just chuckle and smile,
For winter's a joke that lingers awhile.
Embrace the cold, wear your funniest gear,
And dance with the snow, let go of the fear!

The Vanishing Heat

Oh, the warm days, they vanish so fast,
Like a runaway bus, who knew it would pass?
I've lost my sunglasses, where could they be?
In the depths of the closet? Such mysteries, whee!

I cranked up the heat, oh feeling so fine,
Now I'm sweating like a popsicle in line.
The chill creeps back, my joy takes a dip,
My hot cocoa's froze, what a silly trip!

I glance at the forecast, it brings me despair,
It's windy and chilly, oh who thought this fair?
We laughed at the summer, we longed for the cool,
Now winter's here, oh what a fool!

So here's to the heat that just couldn't stay,
And to winter's pranks, all in a day.
We bundle in sweaters, we shiver and play,
As the sun takes its leave, and the frost comes to stay!

Tempest on the Tundra

Under snowflakes, my hat flies away,
Chasing it down, what a comical fray!
I tumble and roll, a frosty ballet,
In the dance of the snow, I lose my display.

The wind howls loudly, like a roaring beast,
I'm caught in a whirlwind, a winter feast!
I laugh with the snowmen, like pals in a row,
While I search for a spot to let out my glow.

The sleds go whizzing, oh what a delight,
I bank off a mound, it’s a comfortable height!
But when I get up, my nose is all red,
The frostbite has shown that it’s recharged my head!

So let’s toast to the tempest, let laughter arise,
For the shivers and slips are a winter's surprise.
We'll cherish the chaos, come heat or come chill,
In the heart of the tundra, we’ll laugh and we will thrill!

A Breath of Ice

In winter's chill, the laughter grows,
A snowman's hat, a nose of hose.
Slipping on ice, oh what a sight,
We tumble and roll, oh what a fright.

Hot cocoa splashed on my friend's new coat,
He shivers and shakes like a chilly goat.
Snowflakes land on our noses and cheeks,
We giggle and snort, it's laughter we seek.

Frost giants dance with their zany moves,
Chasing our shadows, they’ve got the grooves.
With snowball fights, we throw with glee,
But someone just splashed me with hot tea!

As winter ends, we’ll savor this spree,
A breath of ice, oh what fun to be free!

Tales from the Arctic Abyss

The seals wear shades, looking quite fine,
While penguins parade in a snowbird line.
Laughing so loud, the frost starts to sneak,
In the ruckus we lose our boots on a peak.

An ice cream truck with flavors so bold,
Slips on the snow as the story unfolds.
The flavor of mint? Seems a bit cold,
But down a big scoop, we all dare be bold.

One walrus sings high, another sings low,
A cacophony fills the bright, frosty show.
A dance-off erupts on the icy expanse,
As we join in the fray, all in a trance.

From this frosty land, our giggles arise,
Tales of the arctic, where humor lies.

The Snowbound Dilemma

Stuck in a cabin with nowhere to flee,
My socks are mismatched, who cares, let me be!
Outside's a wonder with blizzards and frost,
Inside, our snacks? They've all been lost!

The board games are playing us, it's a mess,
Someone keep rolling, I'm feeling the stress!
A few rounds of charades, laughter did burst,
Until we all froze, and our tongues were cursed.

Ping-ponging snowballs from window to door,
Your aim's getting wild, you've hit me before!
With a sled of dreams, we'll race down the slope,
But first I need snacks, or else there's no hope!

Though snowbound we might be, laughs echo loud,
In this winter's quest, we're merry and proud!

Threads of a Winter Myth

A tale from the tundra, wrapped in a quilt,
Where snowflakes giggle, and ice cakes are built.
A baker's delight, a frosty surprise,
With dough in the air, it flies to the skies!

One frosty cat, with a whisker so grand,
Decides to host parties on snow-covered land.
She puts on a show, with a jolly fat fox,
And dances all night in her warm, cozy socks.

The myths of the winter bring chuckles and cheer,
As squirrels play chess with no hint of fear.
A crooning snowshoe, with stars in her eyes,
Finds treasure in laughter, where friendship lies!

So weave all your stories in snowflakes and sighs,
For here in the winter, the humor won't die!

Glacial Heartbreak

There once was a man in a snowshoe,
Who slipped on a patch of bright blue,
He tumbled and rolled,
His story was told,
As he laughed through each icy skew.

His love was a snowman named Fred,
But he melted away in his bed,
With a sigh and a frown,
He plopped on the ground,
Sipping cocoa while feeling misled.

He found a warm drink in a flask,
And decided to give it a bask,
But the lid would not budge,
So he gave it a grudge,
And threw it right back in the cask.

Now he dances with penguins at night,
Wearing mittens that fit just right,
With a grin on his face,
He twirls with such grace,
In a snowstorm that's silly and bright.

The Perils of Winter's Grasp

A squirrel in a hat made of cheese,
Was trying to dodge winter's freeze,
He slipped on a crust,
With barely a thrust,
And fell with a laugh and a wheeze.

The snowflakes would tickle his nose,
As he danced with his toes and his woes,
With a chuckle so loud,
He attracted a crowd,
Who joined in the frosty repose.

A snowball fight started with flair,
But soon turned to laughter and hair,
That got stuck on a branch,
Oh, what a poor chance,
For sweet squirrels to dance without care.

As twilight descended so brisk,
They decided this moment to risk,
In a pile of white fluff,
With their giggles enough,
To warm hearts with a wintery whisk.

Shattered Icicles

Icicles hung from the roof,
As if dangling a missing tooth,
But one took a dive,
And sadly survived,
A crash that was loud and uncouth.

The dog saw the ice slip and spin,
He jumped with a wag and a grin,
He slipped on the ground,
Then turned all around,
As he barked at the mess and the din.

A snowman was holding its breath,
Afraid it would soon meet its death,
But it just couldn't flee,
It laughed wild and free,
While dodging the cold and a chef.

The chaos was more than just fun,
With snowmen and pups on the run,
In a frenzy and cheer,
For winter's weird year,
What a sight with the cold and the sun!

Battling the Bitter Chill

With mittens too big for her hands,
She marched out to conquer the lands,
But tripped on a mound,
And spun round and round,
While yelling, “This was not in my plans!”

She found herself neck-deep in snow,
With a shovel that wouldn't let go,
As she dug and she scoffed,
While the neighbors just laughed,
At the sight of her wild, snowy glow.

A snow fort was built with great pride,
But her brother took that as a ride,
With a cannon of fluff,
He made things quite rough,
As the flakes flew like starlings worldwide.

And in the end, laughter won,
With cocoa and tales to be spun,
In the warmth of the cheer,
They forgot all the fear,
And melted the chill just for fun.

When Snowflakes Stumble

Snowflakes tumble, oh what a sight,
They twist and they turn, in pure delight.
One hits a nose, another on a hat,
They giggle and wiggle, imagine that!

The ground is a canvas, all white and bright,
Yet one little flake lost its flight.
It drifted too far, caught in a gust,
Landed on a snowman, oh what a bust!

Snowballs fly in a friendly fight,
But someone slipped... oh what a fright!
The laughter erupts, it's all silly fun,
Winter's a playground, oh ain't it run?

So when you see flakes take a fall,
Just chuckle and smile, enjoy it all.
For life’s little stumbles, we all embrace,
With joy and with laughter, in winter's grace.

Frost’s Cruel Embrace

When winter whispers with icy breath,
It’ll tickle your toes while you behold death.
Your mittens go missing, oh what a shame,
For fingers turn blue like it’s part of the game.

Snow drifts are high but boots are low,
And slipping is art in this frosty show.
With every small tumble, a chuckle's made,
As snowmen pop up, they’ve got it made!

A squirrel on a branch, who’s plotting a fall,
Wobbles and fumbles, it’s humorous thrall.
The fluffy white fluff piles high on the lane,
As laughter erupts from the sillies in vain.

So bundle up tight, don’t let it freeze,
Watch out for the frost, oh do it with ease.
Despite the chill’s grip, we’ll do one more dance,
In winter’s warm hug, we’ll rejoice at a chance.

Slippery Shadows

The pavement glimmers, like glass in the sun,
But watch where you step—it's all a big pun!
A slip and a slide, oh what a delight,
With arms windmilling, your balance is light!

Children are laughing, they fly with the breeze,
With every fun fall, they're down on their knees.
But behold the grown-ups, so careful and grand,
Yet somehow they tumble, just can't make a stand!

Snowflakes dance softly in the glow of the night,
While shadows emerge, causing laughter to ignite.
Chasing their footprints, like kids in a dream,
The cold brings a chuckle, or so it would seem!

So here's to the slips, the falls that we share,
When winter rolls in, with its frosty affair.
We laugh till we cry, oh what a wild show,
In slippery shadows where giggles still flow.

A Dance with the Cold

In a swirling ballet of snow and of frost,
We twirl and we spin, never counting the cost.
With cheeks rosy red and noses aglow,
We glide with the chill, oh how we do flow!

The wind joins the party, it whispers and shouts,
As scarves go a-flailing, all twirls and no doubts.
With mittens a-flapping, we trip and we cheer,
Winter's a dance that we hearty souls steer!

But suddenly 'whoops!' a misstep from Bob,
He landed in snow while he tried for a job.
We roll on the ground, our laughter does rise,
This dance with the cold brings tears to our eyes!

So let's raise a toast to this frosty ballet,
With each little slip, we seize the next play.
Embrace all the giggles, the slips we ignore,
In this waltz of pure joy, we all ask for more!

Resilience of the Winter's Heart

The snowflakes dance, a merry crew,
My fingers numb, but I laugh, it's true.
A snowman grins with a carrot nose,
Yet all around him, the chaos grows.

The hot cocoa spills while I cheerfully slip,
Against the icy ground, I grimly grip.
The winter sun shines, so bright, so bold,
But I can't feel my toes, or so I'm told.

Sledding down hills with a yelp and a cheer,
But landing in snowdrifts, oh dear, oh dear!
The laughter rings loud, despite the chill,
As I try to stand up, I tumble down still.

Through blizzards we march, with hats on our heads,
But secretly hoping for warm, cozy beds.
Each frosty mishap, a tale to narrate,
In winter's embrace, we find joy—it's great!

Buried in the Snowdrift

A jump into snow, a wild surprise,
Face full of white, oh where are my eyes?
The kids all laugh, in their snowball fight,
While I dig for my boot, buried out of sight.

I build a fine castle, all tall and grand,
But one rogue snowman has made a stand.
He lops off the tower, with a chilly snicker,
And I start to whine—oh please, not thicker!

The hot chocolate flows, but the fridge is frozen,
Every sip I take feels like a game chosen.
With marshmallows bobbing, a fluffy delight,
I laugh loud and snort—what a frosty plight!

In the snowdrift’s arms, I sink and I roll,
Finding my joy in the winter's cold thrall.
With jackets all zipped, we bundle up tight,
In the chaos of winter, I feel so light!

Cascade of Frozen Regrets

In a blizzard of choices, I trudge through the day,
Each step like a dance on the edge of ballet.
The ice on my path tells tales of defeat,
Yet it's hard not to chuckle at my own two left feet.

I thought I could glide, a pro on the sled,
But the way that I flopped—it’s best left unsaid.
My friends all took photos, with glee in their eyes,
While I laid in a heap, yelling, 'I’m off to the skies!'

The snowflakes just giggle, they know what I lack,
While I try to find warmth, my nose turns to black.
I swear they are plotting, those sparkly bits,
As I trip on the path full of slippery fits.

Yet in all this clamor and chaos so bold,
I find joy is made from the stories retold.
Each tumble and splash is a memory dear,
In winter's wild folly, I shed my cold fear!

Ghosts of Frozen Nights

Long nights of shivering under stars so bright,
I hear the wind howling, oh what a fright!
But igloos of laughter fill cold, dark spaces,
Where marshmallow specters hold hot cocoa races.

The frost bites my nose while I warm up my hands,
Telling spooky stories as the moonlight stands.
Each tale that we share brings a laugh or a scream,
As we sip from our mugs with a frosty sheen.

The ghosts of the snowmen come join in the fun,
With their top hats and scarves, they dance one by one.
We frolic and fall, in this wintery state,
And share in the blunders that we can't, but relate.

When morning dawns bright, it's all laughter and cheer,
The ice ghosts retreat, but they'll soon reappear.
With each frozen night, we remember we're bold,
For the warmth is our laughter and the stories we've told!

The Frost's Lament

The ground is cold, my toes complain,
With every step, I feel the pain.
A slip, a slide, a flurry of snow,
I laugh it off, but oh, no more!

The icicles dangle, a sharp little threat,
As I dodge them, my shoes are all wet.
Oh winter, you jester, so full of cheer,
You bring us joy mixed with icy fear!

My fingers are numb, they wave goodbye,
To warmth and comfort, oh how they cry!
But the snowman smiles with a carrot nose,
It’s hard to frown with such silly pose!

So here’s to the chill, the giggles we share,
With slip-ups and tumbles, life’s never rare.
Each frosty mishap, a story anew,
We chuckle and chortle, like winter’s own crew!

Whispers of the Icebound Heart

The wind whispers secrets, a chilling tale,
Of penguin-like waddles and many a fail.
With snowflakes dancing, I trip on a mound,
Then roll like an otter, round and round!

My cheeks are rosy, my breath makes a cloud,
I'm an ice-skater now, proud and loud.
But my moves are more awkward than elegant grace,
Like a penguin in boots, I quicken my pace!

Hot cocoa waiting, a tempting delight,
But first, I must conquer this frosty fight.
A tumble and giggle, a slip, not a fall,
The ice is a prankster, but I'll have a ball!

So here in the freeze, the laughter is bright,
With snowball fights and chattering bites.
Each frosty adventure, a chuckle to share,
In this winter wonder, with giggles in the air!

The Frosty Encounter

Stomp on the ground, feel the crunch,
A frosty encounter, time for a munch.
A snowflake flutters, lands on my nose,
I sneeze like a cartoon, oh how it goes!

I build a snowman, he’s rather stout,
With a scarf and a hat, no doubt about.
But he leans too far, gives one silly smile,
As I laugh and he topples, oh, what a trial!

The slippery sidewalk, a jester's delight,
I dance 'round the edges, try to be light.
But down I go, like a clumsy old bear,
With giggles erupting, no worry, no care!

Through frost-filled adventures, with folly so sweet,
The cold may be harsh, but can’t take my beat.
In snow-covered mischief, we find our own spark,
In each frosty moment, we leave our mark!

Echoes of the Winter Wall

The wall stands tall, wrapped in white,
I hurl my snowball with all of my might.
But the wall just chuckles, absorbs my throw,
And I’m left standing, feeling quite slow.

I challenge the frost, with a bravado so bold,
Yet the ice has its plans, and my story’s retold.
I leap and I spin, but oh, what a flop,
As I crumple in snow, it’s a hilarious drop!

My friends gather 'round, laughter in sight,
With each futile attempt, the mood feels just right.
We roll in the snow, like happy old bears,
Creating a ruckus, without any cares!

So here in the cold, where giggles abound,
Each frosty blunder is joyously crowned.
We’re wrapped in our blankets, as night starts to fall,
By echoes of laughter around winter's wall!

Tread Lightly on Ice

Waddling like a penguin, I take my stance,
Hoping to avoid the icy dance.
With every careful step I try to glide,
But down I go, arms flailing wide!

Laughter bursts from all around,
As I perform a frosty face plant sound.
Snowflakes fall, they join the fun,
A winter trip, not quite a run!

Cautious moves and silly slips,
I navigate these frozen trips.
A comedy of winter woes,
As I strike a pose or two, who knows?

Yet when the sun begins to shine,
I search for warmth, a chance divine.
But shiny ice, it still remains,
My prize for fun and frozen pains!

Shadows in the Winter Light

In the glow of the sun, shadows dance,
I step forward, it feels like a chance.
But the ground gives way, oh what a sight,
My shadow laughs, it’s out of fright!

People gather, I hear their cheer,
As I tumble down, it's crystal clear.
A slip and slide on this icy stage,
Turns winter's chill into a laughing rage.

Snowflakes twirl with a comic grace,
While I attempt to reclaim my place.
It’s me against ice, what a plight,
Chasing shadows in the winter light!

But at the end of this curvy ride,
I find my smile, no longer hide.
For every slip, there’s laughter to find,
In this wintry world, oh so unkind!

The Frigid Fumble

With boots so big, I think I’ll glide,
But gravity calls, and I can’t abide.
A fumble here, a slide there,
My chilly exit, full of flair!

Children giggle, dogs chase my hat,
As I roll around, just like that.
The world's a game—no need to fret,
With frosty tumbles, I won’t forget!

Snowballs fly in a friendly fight,
I toss one back, with all my might.
But on the ice, my fate unseals,
A splendid crash, it’s how it feels!

Still, joy abounds in winter’s jest,
Where slips and giggles never rest.
For in this cold, we’re all the same,
In laughter's warmth, we find our fame!

Slips of the Heart

On a frozen heart, I take a chance,
Hoping to impress with some cool dance.
But oh, the irony, it hits me hard,
As I land flat in the backyard!

The cat just smirks, all warm and sleek,
While I lay there, not a word to speak.
My heart may slip, but so does pride,
When icy love's around to provide!

Yet still I rise, with dreams anew,
To skate on feelings, fresh and blue.
Every thud fuels my brave new start,
In this comical game of slips of the heart.

So here I go, let laughter reign,
With every fall, there's joy to gain.
For life's a slippery, frosty art,
Where every turn is a trick of the heart!

Milton Keynes UK
Ingram Content Group UK Ltd.
UKHW021951151124
451186UK00007B/190

9 789916 943229